EVERYDAY LIFE IN

ANCIENT GREECE

ANNE PEARSON

W
FRANKLIN WATTS
LONDON • SYDNEY

This edition published in 2003 by
Franklin Watts
96 Leonard Street
London EC2A 4XD

Franklin Watts Australia
45-51 Huntley Street
Alexandria
NSW 2015

© 1993 Franklin Watts

ISBN 0 7496 2036 6

A CIP catalogue record for this book is available
from the British Library.

Editor: Sarah Ridley
Designer: Alan Cassedy
Illustrator: Ed Dovey
Picture researcher: Joanne King

Photographs: Ancient Art and Architecture Library
4t, 24t, 24b, 25b;
the Trustees of the British Museum front cover bl and br, 8t,
10t, 12t, 16t, 18t, 20t, 22t, 26t, 30t;
Werner Forman Archive 28t; Michael Holford 6(all), 7(all), 14t.

Printed in Dubai, UAE

CONTENTS

The land of Greece is made up of high mountains, valleys and open plains, all surrounded by a jagged coastline. The earliest great civilisation in the area of Greece was that of the Minoans, so-called after their legendary king, Minos. Its centre was the island of Crete which became very rich and powerful.

When the Minoan civilisation came to an end a new power grew up, this time on the Greek mainland. A war-like people, called Mycenaeans, ruled over Greece and traded far and wide in the Mediterranean.

After the Mycenaean period, there were a few hundred years when there were no powerful rulers and little foreign trade. This time is sometimes called the Dark Ages. It came to an end in the 8th century BC when Greeks started to travel abroad again and establish new colonies.

Back in Greece, the city states grew rich because of their overseas trade and success in war. Some cities, especially Athens, became rich and powerful and reached a peak of civilisation in the classical period in the mid-5th century BC.

The next great power in Greece was Macedonia in the north. Alexander the Great defeated the Persian Empire and created a vast empire, spreading Greek civilisation far beyond the lands around the Aegean Sea.

This gold mask was found by archaeologists at Mycenae and must have belonged to a Mycenaean king. It is sometimes called the mask of Agamemnon and is dated 1550-1500 BC.

IMPORTANT DATES FROM THE TIME OF THE ANCIENT GREEKS

2000-1500 BC

Minoan palace civilisation (Bronze Age). Palace of Knossos built. Fall of Knossos and rise of Mycenaean civilisation.

1500-1100 BC

The rise of the Mycenaeans. Invasion of Crete. Trojan War. Collapse of Mycenaean civilisation.

1100-800 BC

The rise of the city states. The Dark Ages.

800-600 BC

The Homeric poems. Colonies founded. **776** First Olympic Games held. First coins introduced. Introduction of the alphabet.

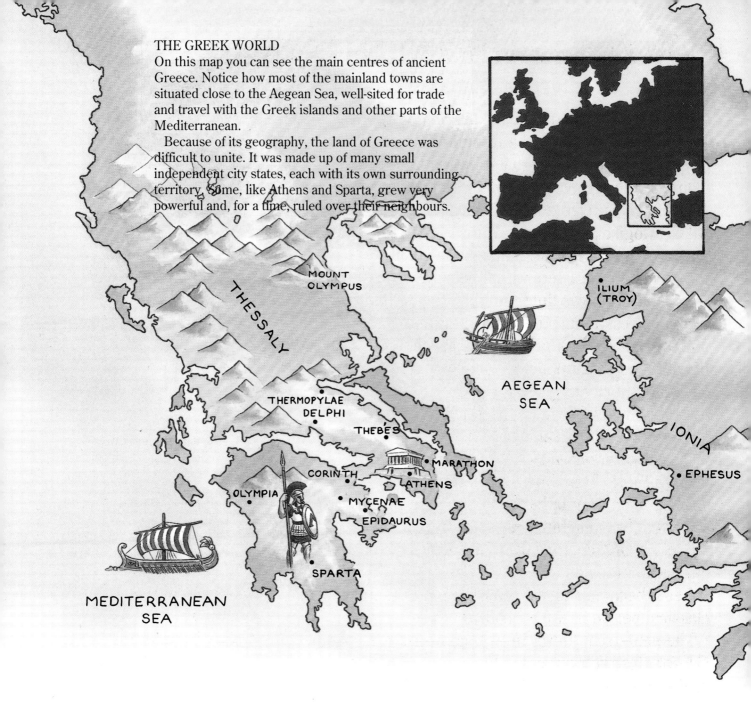

THE GREEK WORLD

On this map you can see the main centres of ancient Greece. Notice how most of the mainland towns are situated close to the Aegean Sea, well-sited for trade and travel with the Greek islands and other parts of the Mediterranean.

Because of its geography, the land of Greece was difficult to unite. It was made up of many small independent city states, each with its own surrounding territory. Some, like Athens and Sparta, grew very powerful and, for a time, ruled over their neighbours.

THESSALY

MOUNT OLYMPUS

ILIUM (TROY)

AEGEAN SEA

THERMOPYLAE
DELPHI

THEBES

IONIA

MARATHON

CORINTH

ATHENS

EPHESUS

OLYMPIA

MYCENAE

EPIDAURUS

SPARTA

MEDITERRANEAN SEA

600-480 BC

Beginnings of democracy in Athens.
Beginnings of tragedy and comedy.
490-479 Persian wars.

480-400 BC

Age of Pericles.
447-432 Parthenon built at Athens.
The Classical period.
431-404 War between Athens and Sparta.

400-300 BC

Rise of Philip of Macedon.
336 Death of Philip and succession of Alexander the Great.

336-323 Alexander wins empire stretching from Egypt to northern India.
323 Death of Alexander.

The ancient Greeks have left behind them clues that tell us about their daily life. We know about them from reading their literature, from the impressive buildings which still stand today and from the evidence of archaeological excavation. You can see Greek objects, especially vases and sculpture, in many museums around the world.

Our culture owes much to the Greeks. Poetry, drama, philosophy, politics, science and medicine, architecture and art have all been influenced by them.

This Greek sculpture of a beautiful young man is one of a number which have survived. It may represent the god Apollo, and it shows how much Greek artists admired the human body. It was their favourite subject.

STANDING STRUCTURES

Some of the most famous temples can be seen on the Acropolis, a high rocky plateau which dominates the city of Athens. It was a sacred area in classical times but before that was a place of safety where Athenians could retreat if they were under attack.

Another important Greek site is Delphi, the sacred place of Apollo. Archaeologists have discovered a stadium and temples there, as well as roads. Delphi was thought by the Greeks to be the centre of the world and a huge stone called the *omphalos*, or navel of the world, has been found there.

These amazing buildings give us a sense of the power and majesty of Greek civilisation. Because of the genius of the architects and sculptors, their work has survived the passing of time and the ravages of earthquakes, wind and rain.

The Acropolis, Athens

ARCHAEOLOGY

Archaeologists have excavated many sites and the results can tell us much about ordinary life in the ancient Greek world. Bits of pottery, metalwork and sometimes jewellery have been found, as well as the foundations of buildings. The soil in Greece is not dry enough for fabrics and wood to survive so our knowledge of clothes and furniture comes mainly from the illustrations on Greek pots.

POTTERY

We know a great deal about life in ancient Greece from the pictures painted on Greek vases. They show clothes, furniture and people going about their everyday life. Many of these pots have been dug up out of the soil, or found in tombs where they had been left with the dead person as offerings to the gods.

LITERATURE

This is a sculpture of Homer who composed the two long poems, the *Iliad* and the *Odyssey*, in the 8th century BC. Greek authors wrote on paper made from a tall reed called papyrus and few of their papyrus scrolls have survived. However, it was the Romans who saved the knowledge and art of Greek scientists, philosophers and writers for later times by making many copies of the Greek books they obtained when they absorbed Greece into their empire.

8 FARMING AND FISHING

Many scenes showing everyday life were painted on to Greek pots. This one shows farmworkers gathering olives. One man has climbed the tree and others shake the branches with sticks. The olives fall to the ground and are collected in baskets. Olive trees grew well in the dry sandy soil of Greece, as they still do today. This pot is an amphora and was used for storing wine and keeping it cool. It was made in Athens about 520 BC.

FARMING AND HUNTING

Most people in Greece were farmers. Their farming year began in October when the land was ploughed using a wooden plough and seeds were scattered in the furrows. In spring, the ripe barley or wheat was harvested and later used to make porridge and bread. Farmers usually kept sheep and goats on the hills around them and a few dairy cows too, if the land was fertile enough.

On the higher ground, exposed to the sun, were the vineyards. Here the grapes were grown to make wine, the favourite drink of the Greeks, especially the rich ones. Poorer people drank goats' milk and water.

Rich young men went hunting for wild deer and boar which they would eat on special occasions, perhaps a festival in honour of a god or goddess. Most of the time people did not eat much meat. Fish, however, was plentiful and many Greek settlements were quite close to the sea.

This beautiful dish is painted with pictures of fish. It was probably used for serving real fish, such as mackerel and mullet, squid and eel. The hollow in the middle was for a rich spicy sauce.

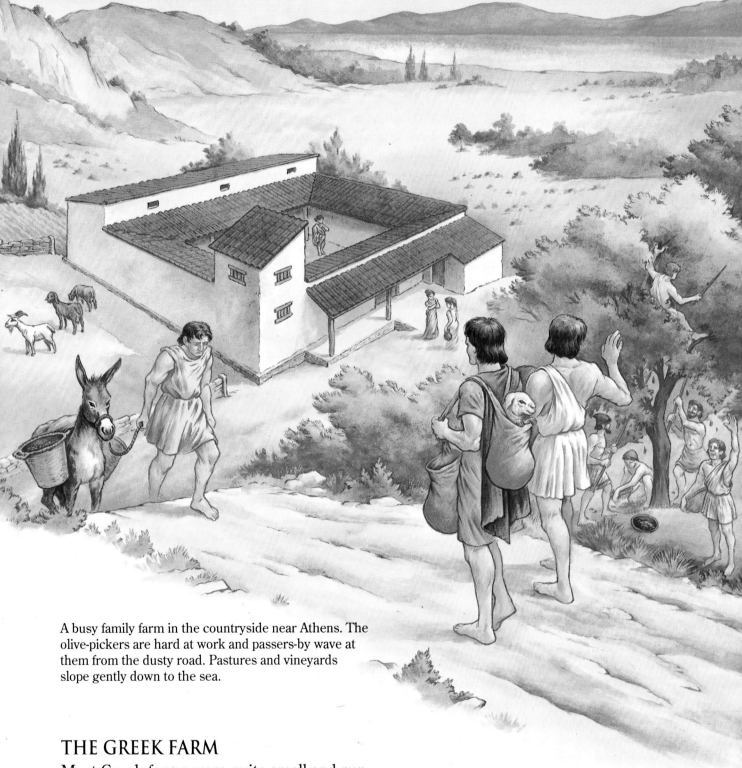

A busy family farm in the countryside near Athens. The olive-pickers are hard at work and passers-by wave at them from the dusty road. Pastures and vineyards slope gently down to the sea.

THE GREEK FARM

Most Greek farms were quite small and run by one family with a few farmhands and slaves. Some richer people who lived in Athens had farms in the countryside nearby which were managed for them by bailiffs.

Beans, lentils, onions and carrots were the main vegetable crops and farmers also kept pigs and hens in the farmyard. Donkeys were important for transporting the goods to market. Weighed down with panniers filled with cheeses, jars of wine and olive oil they made regular journeys into town.

Farmhouses, like town houses, were built around a central courtyard. Some of them had defensive towers built to protect them from attack during times of war.

The Greeks liked to drink their wine with plenty of water. Boys would mix the water and wine together in a big bowl like this one. The bowls were perched on painted clay stands placed conveniently close to the drinkers so that they could refill their cups at ease. This famous bowl was painted by the artist Sophilos. Around the very top of the bowl, Sophilos has painted a long procession of gods and goddesses. They are all going to the wedding of a couple called Peleus and Thetis. Vase painters often painted scenes from mythology on the surface of wine bowls.

THE HOUSE

Because of the hot climate the Greeks spent a great deal of time out of doors. Their houses always had a central courtyard where the children could play while the women did their spinning out of the sun. A flight of steps led to the upper floor where the bedrooms and servants' quarters were.

The roof of the house had clay tiles and the walls were made of mud brick. Windows were small and had wooden shutters which were fastened in the winter. The doors were also made of wood which was expensive because it was in short supply. Outside the main door of the house there was often a statue, called a *herm*, of the messenger god, Hermes. It was placed there to protect the family from evil spirits. Floors were made of beaten earth and colourful woven hangings covered the walls.

LIGHTING
Small clay or bronze lamps gave a flickering light at night. They were fuelled by olive oil and must have been a bit smoky. They were used mainly at evening parties. Most people probably went to bed when the sun went down.

Men recline on couches at an evening party. The slave girl keeps them supplied with food and drink.

Furniture was usually made of wood, sometimes inlaid with decorations of ivory or metal. Couches used for reclining to eat were similar in design to those on which people slept. They were covered in cushions and colourful blankets. The tables were low enough to be pushed underneath the couches. There were also chests, boxes and baskets where personal items like perfume bottles, spindles and toys were kept.

Chair

Table

Stool

THE ANDRON

Men and women had separate areas inside the house. The men often entertained their friends and business associates at drinking parties in the *andron*, the men's area, where they reclined on couches and were served by slave boys and girls. The *andron* was often near the entrance to the house so that the guests leaving the party in a drunken state would not run the risk of offending a woman member of the household.

A woman would have placed this clay object over her knee to provide a surface for teasing out wool. Called an *epinetron*, it is beautifully decorated with painted scenes of women working at home. The painting shows how the woman would pull the wool across the *epinetron*, drawing out thin strands which were then suitable for spinning. Spinning and weaving were regarded as important tasks for women, even for the high-born and wealthy ones.

WOMEN IN THE HOUSE

In most Greek homes there was a special room called the *gynaekonitis* where the women gathered to work, entertain their friends and be with their children. Here the looms were kept along with the baskets of wool and spindles. The women made the clothes for the family as well as curtains and covers for the couches. Only exotic silks, braids and borders were bought ready-made from the market.

The lives of Greek women were spent mainly in the home. They could not take part in politics and rarely had a job in the outside world. Girls got married about the age of thirteen to husbands who were usually much older, in their twenties or thirties. A girl's father usually chose her husband for her and gave a dowry to the bridegroom – a gift of money and possessions.

Some women may have been taught about writers and poets, as well as arithmetic and they could handle the family finances. They may have had quite a lot of power and influence in the home.

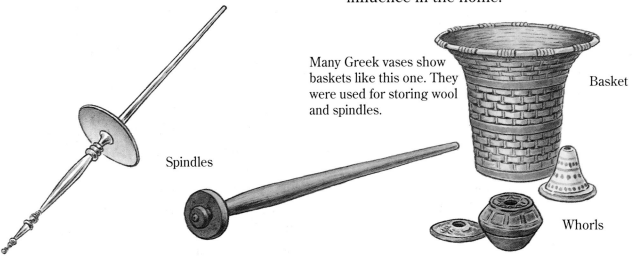

Spindles

Many Greek vases show baskets like this one. They were used for storing wool and spindles.

Basket

Whorls

Three young wives work together making cloth with spindle, loom and *epinetron*.

Very many perfume pots and containers for combs and cosmetics have been found by archaeologists on Greek sites. This suggests that Greek women liked to use make-up. It was not fashionable to have a suntan and creams were used to protect the skin. Make-up created a pale look.

SPINDLES, DISTAFFS AND LOOMS

When the wool had been dyed, cleaned and combed it was ready to be spun. A woman would use her spindle, a long pointed stick, for this. In her left hand she would hold a distaff with the clump of wool on it. The women would draw a woollen thread from the distaff onto the spindle and then let the spindle drop towards the ground, twisting the thread as it went.

The prepared thread was woven on an upright loom. The looms were propped up against the wall and the women stood in front of them to weave.

Greek clothes were loose and flowing, as shown on this terracotta (fired clay) figure of a woman. She is wearing a tunic called a chiton, with a cloak called a himation over the top. Many terracotta figures have been found. They were made as ornaments for the home or as religious offerings in the temples. When they were new they would have been brightly painted, but these colours have nearly always disappeared.

CLOTHES FOR MEN AND WOMEN

Both men and women wore the chiton. It was made by fastening or tying together a rectangular piece of woollen or linen cloth, leaving gaps for the head and arms. It was gathered in at the waist with a soft belt. Chitons were often dyed pretty colours, such as saffron yellow or red.

MYSTERY
O B J E C T

What do you think these are? They were found in the women's room, near make-up containers. Clue: they would have smelt pleasant. You will find the answer on page 32.

The chiton was usually long, reaching down to the ankles, but working men, slaves and children wore shorter, knee-length ones, leaving them freer to work or play. Over the top of the chiton people wore a large cloak called a himation which often had decorated borders. These clothes were very light and cool, making them suitable for the hot Greek climate.

HAIRSTYLES AND HEADGEAR

Unless they were slaves, women wore their hair very long. Before they were married they wore it in long ringlets, but after that they piled it up on their heads with ribbons and metal hair decorations. When they went out they pulled their cloaks up over their heads. Men sometimes wore a wide hat of straw or fabric to protect them from the sun when travelling.

A Greek family wearing the clothes of the time. The slave (left) wears a short tunic so that he can move about quickly and easily.

Rich women wore a lot of gold and silver jewellery, especially dangly ear-rings, bracelets and rings. Men wore rings on their fingers too and fastened their cloaks with big brooches.

Can you guess what this is? It is actually a clay rattle in the shape of a pig. Bits of clay were sealed inside to make it rattle. Probably only the children of well-off families who lived in towns would have been given toys like this to play with. A number of clay toys, especially dolls and puppets, have been found in the graves of children, put there to take with them to the next world.

CHILDHOOD

On Greek vases babies can sometimes be seen being cuddled by their mothers or sitting in clay high chairs, which were also potties. However, only the strong babies were given the chance to survive into childhood. If a baby was very weak, its father might decide to let it die by leaving it out in the cold. Sometimes these babies were rescued and brought up as slaves.

GROWING UP

The quality of a child's life very much depended on how rich its parents were. The sons and daughters of poor farmers worked hard from their early years, scaring birds from crops and helping with the harvest.

At about the age of twelve, children were regarded as having grown up. There was a special religious ceremony for them, welcoming them to adult life. Boys and girls brought their toys to the temple and left them there as offerings to the god Apollo and his twin sister, Artemis.

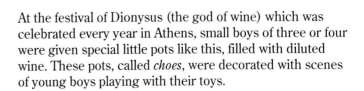

At the festival of Dionysus (the god of wine) which was celebrated every year in Athens, small boys of three or four were given special little pots like this, filled with diluted wine. These pots, called *choes*, were decorated with scenes of young boys playing with their toys.

Children playing with their terracotta spinning tops, dolls and rattles.

GAMES

Greek children played many of the games that children play today – blindman's buff, tag, spinning tops, hoops and ball games of all kinds using a ball made out of a pig's bladder. They also played throwing and guessing games with dice and counters made out of stone and the knucklebones of small animals.

They kept pets such as cats, dogs and hares and some even had little wooden go-carts which were pulled along by goats. These can sometimes be seen on the *choes*.

These clay toys would have been brightly coloured when they were new. Faint traces of original paint sometimes survive.

GOING TO SCHOOL

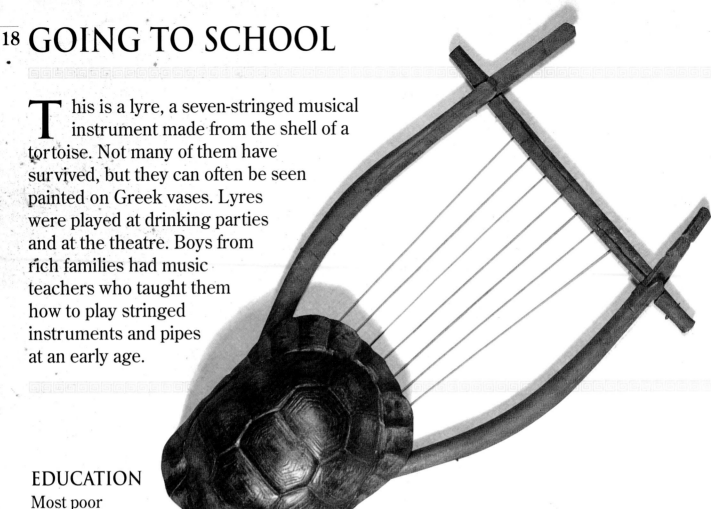

This is a lyre, a seven-stringed musical instrument made from the shell of a tortoise. Not many of them have survived, but they can often be seen painted on Greek vases. Lyres were played at drinking parties and at the theatre. Boys from rich families had music teachers who taught them how to play stringed instruments and pipes at an early age.

EDUCATION

Most poor children hardly had any education at all and probably never learnt to read and write. For the better off there were schools in Athens and other cities in ancient Greece, but they were only for boys. Girls were usually taught at home by their mothers. They learnt how to spin and weave and how to run the household, but some girls from wealthier families were also taught to read and write.

Boys learnt the works of famous poets, such as Homer, off by heart. A knowledge of Greek literature was the sign of an educated man. Sport and games were also an important part of a boy's education. These skills helped them to be tough soldiers in adult life.

WRITING MATERIALS

The pupils wrote with a sharp pen called a stylus which was made of bone or metal. They wrote on wooden tablets covered in wax. When they made a mistake they would rub it out using the other blunt end of the stylus. The teacher would read aloud to them from a scroll made of paper from the papyrus plant.

Papyrus scroll and stylus

SCHOOL

Boys started going to school at the age of
seven. So that they could not play truant,
they were usually taken to and from school
by a slave tutor. Classes would have had
only eight or nine pupils sitting on stools
around their teacher. They were taught
reading, writing and arithmetic and used
pebbles and a special wired frame called an
abacus to help them count. Classes were
held only in the morning. In the afternoon
the boys practised athletics.

The teacher sits surrounded by his pupils, showing
them a papyrus scroll. In the background, an older boy
is plucking a lyre.

THE ALPHABET

The Phoenicians, a people who traded with the Greeks,
brought the alphabet to Greece in about 800 BC. More
letters were added and it soon became widely used by
all educated people. Here is a line in Greek from a play
by a famous writer called Aeschylus. It means,
  "I have brought you up, and want to grow old with
you beside me."

A	B	Γ	Δ	E	Z
A	B	G	D	E	Z

H	Θ	I	K	Λ	M
EE	TH	I	K	L	M

N	Ξ	O	Π	P	Σ
N	X/KS	O	P	R	S

T	Y	Φ	X	Ψ	Ω
T	U	F/PH	CH	PS	OH

ἐγώ σ' ἐθρεψα,
συν δε γηραναι
θελω

A cobbler is shown here on this drinking cup, sitting at his work bench and cutting up pieces of leather. Hanging on hooks on the wall behind him are the tools of his craft and some of the boots and sandals he has made. In the towns of ancient Greece there were many small craftsmen like this man; metalworkers, jewellers, ivory carvers and, most numerous of all, potters.

POTTERY

The best Greek pottery was made in the city of Athens. The potters worked together in small groups of five or six people, usually men, although some women were also involved, especially in painting the pots.

There was a room where they made the pots, sometimes with the help of a slave who turned the wheel. When the pots were dry and firm they painted them with a clay solution using fine brushes. This clay solution changed colour to a shiny black while the pots were being fired in the kiln.

An adjoining room served as a shop where customers came to buy household jars, cups and crockery.

Greek pots are often painted with beautiful scenes of everyday life and events in the lives of the gods and heroes. Because the fired clay survives so well, many museums today have large collections of Greek pottery.

NAMES OF SOME POT SHAPES:

Amphora – two-handled jar for storing wine
Krater – large pot for mixing water and wine
Kylix – wide drinking cup with two handles
Oinochoe – wine jug

Amphora

Oinochoe

Kylix

Krater

A thrifty Greek housewife measures out the cloth carefully before making her purchase in the agora.

THE AGORA

Every Greek town had an agora, or market place, where people came everyday to do the household shopping, meet friends or do business. It was a large open space near the centre of town, with surrounding colonnades, beneath which stalls were set up. Here the vegetables, cheeses, olives and fruit, brought in by donkey-cart from the country farms, were sold. Here, too, more expensive items, such as footwear, ear-rings and fine clothes and cloth for special occasions, could be purchased.

MONEY

Coins came to Greece in the late 7th century BC from Lydia in Asia Minor where they were invented. Each city state minted its own coins of gold, silver and electrum (a mixture of silver and gold).

At first coins were too valuable to be used in everyday transactions and ordinary people continued to barter and exchange goods with each other. Later, coins made of a cheaper metal, bronze, were used for shopping in the market place.

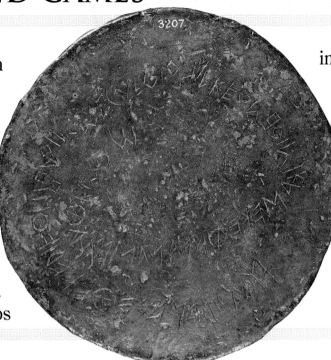

We know from this bronze discus that it belonged to an athlete called Exoidas. His name is written on it along with the information that he won a competition with it. Afterwards, perhaps in thanksgiving, he offered it to Castor and Pollux, the twin sons of the great god Zeus. Discus-throwing was a popular Greek sport, along with javelin-throwing, wrestling, jumping and running.

THE GREEK GAMES

Big sporting festivals, called Games, were held in various parts of Greece in honour of particular gods and goddesses. The most famous were the Olympic Games held at Olympia in honour of Zeus, and the Panathenaic Games, held in Athens in honour of Athena.

These were both held with great splendour every four years, and men came from all over the Greek world to participate and watch. They were important public holidays. As the Greek states were often at war with each other, a truce was called to allow the Olympic Games to be held. That way, all the athletes and spectators could travel safely to and from Olympia.

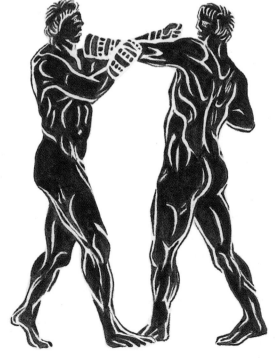

PRIZES

Because the Games were religious occasions and the athletes were competing in honour of the god, they did not receive cash prizes for coming first. The prize for winning a race at Olympia was an olive wreath, but at Athens successful athletes would be awarded olive oil inside a big pot. On one side of the pot there was a picture of the event that had been won. On this one (left), two boxers are fighting each other. Instead of gloves they wear leather thongs wrapped around their fists. The other side of the pot has a painting of the goddess Athena herself.

Athletes exercise in the open air preparing themselves for the Olympic Games.

CONTESTANTS

Boys were taught sporting skills to help them become fit soldiers in adult life. There were special training grounds and wrestling schools in most Greek towns where the boys went to exercise and compete.

Young men took part in the Games naked. At Olympia, the running races and most other events took place on a race-course called the stadium which was about 190 metres long and covered with sand. Many thousands of spectators watched the events from the raised bank along the stadium.

Women were not allowed to take part in the Games. At Olympia however there was a special festival for women in honour of Hera, the wife of Zeus. At this, girls competed against each other in running races.

MYSTERY
O B J E C T

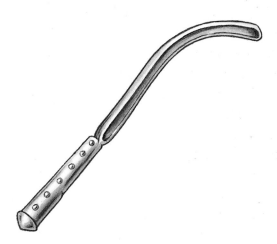

What do you think this object is? It is made of metal and has a handle and a curved edge. It was used by athletes after competing. You will find the answer on page 32.

Can you guess what this object is? It is a theatrical mask made of baked clay and would have been used as a decoration. Similar masks, made of stiffened linen, were worn by actors at the Greek theatre. The mouths were always very large and this allowed the voice of the actor to carry right to the back of the theatre. The expression on the face showed the sort of character the actor was playing.

THE PLAYS

The theatre in Athens began in early times with hymns and dances to the god of wine, Dionysus, for a good grape harvest. Then the plays became an important part of the spring festival of that god. They were either tragedies or types of comedy and as they were always about famous legends and myths, the audience nearly always knew what would happen. They enjoyed watching how different playwrights told the same stories. The plays were judged on this and prizes given to the winners.

We still have copies of plays by four very famous Greek playwrights. Aeschylus, Sophocles and Euripides wrote the serious plays (tragedies) about the mythical past, and Aristophanes wrote comedies which poked fun at the gods and at the politicians of the day.

A theatre survives almost intact at Epidaurus in Greece. Its auditorium with stone seats could take 14,000 people. Modern performances of Greek plays are often held there.

The large circular space in the middle of the theatre was known as the orchestra. Behind it was a building from which the actors came on and off and where they could change into their costumes. Important members of the audience, like the judges, had the best seats near the front.

A BIG DAY OUT

Going to the theatre was an important event in the lives of the ancient Greeks, especially in Athens. The theatre could hold over 10,000 people. Men spent the whole day there, watching three plays, one after another. They took a packed lunch in with them and their own cushions to sit on. Poor people could get free tickets. Only three actors at a time were allowed to speak but there was a chorus of actors who would describe the action on and off stage. Because of the shape of the theatres the sound quality was very good and everyone could hear easily.

These masks have been reconstructed to show how theatrical masks would have looked in Greek times. The mask is made from stiffened linen, with real hair used for the beard and head, and holes for the eyes and mouth.

IN THE ARMY

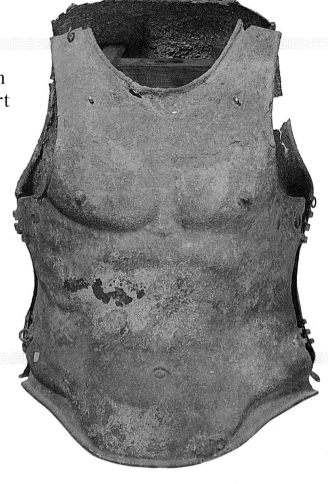

A Greek infantry soldier would have worn this breastplate to protect the upper part of his body in battle. It is made of two bronze plates, moulded to look like the human body and fastened at the sides with leather straps. The Greek soldier who fought on foot was called a hoplite after the *hopla*, shield. He usually had to pay for his own equipment. Along with the breastplate this included his round shield which was made of bronze, like his high-crested helmet. Sometimes hoplites also wore leg guards called greaves.

BATTLE TACTICS

Hoplites fought close together, shoulder to shoulder, in a battle formation called a phalanx, usually eight ranks deep and protected by a wall of shields. They would move towards the enemy and then engage in hand-to-hand combat.

For a long time hoplites were greatly feared all over the eastern Mediterranean, defeating all foreign forces. In 490 BC, the hoplites defeated the invading Persians spectacularly. They routed the invading army – thousands of Persians were killed and the rest were chased back to their ships.

Other Greek soldiers included cavalrymen and auxiliary soldiers, poor men who could not afford hoplite armour. They were sometimes used to protect the hoplite phalanx.

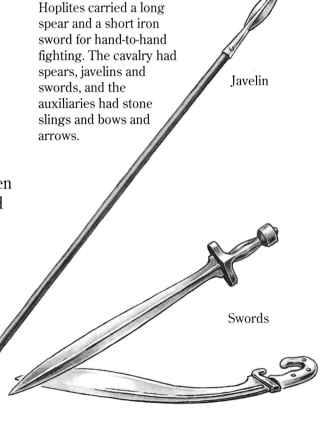

Hoplites carried a long spear and a short iron sword for hand-to-hand fighting. The cavalry had spears, javelins and swords, and the auxiliaries had stone slings and bows and arrows.

Javelin

Swords

The scene above of a young woman saying a tender goodbye to her husband and his friend as they go off to war, must have been very common in real life.

THE LIFE OF A SOLDIER

In Athens and other Greek cities, boys trained to be soldiers between the ages of eighteen and twenty. After that they could be called up when necessary to fight for their city state. War was a normal part of Greek life and battles took place almost every year.

Only the city of Sparta, for a long time the enemy of Athens, had a professional army. The life of the Spartan soldier was very hard. Boys were taught to be tough. They were taken from their families as early as the age of seven and had

to live in freezing cold barracks and eat a horrible black soup. An Athenian writer said that he was not surprised that the Spartans were so brave in battle, because a man would prefer to be killed rather than live such a hard life!

Helmets came in different shapes. This one is of the Corinthian type. Made of bronze, it covers the entire head except for the eyes and mouth. It has a strip of metal to protect the nose.

The most famous Greek temple is the Parthenon. It was built on the Acropolis in Athens between 447 and 432 BC and was decorated with sculptures by the famous Pheidias, a close friend of Pericles, the leader of Athens. The word Parthenon comes from the Greek word *parthenos*, meaning virgin.

GODS AND GODDESSES

The Greeks worshipped many gods. The twelve most important ones were believed to live on the top of a high mountain in northern Greece called Mount Olympus.

Zeus was the king of the gods, and he carried a thunderbolt to symbolise his power over the heavens. He had a wife called Hera, a protector of women and marriage. Poseidon, the brother of Zeus, was god of the sea and carried a trident. Athena, the beautiful grey-eyed daughter of Zeus, was a goddess of wisdom as well as being the patron goddess of the city of Athens. Other deities included Dionysus, the god of wine, Ares, who was god of war, Apollo, god of poetry and the arts, and his twin sister, Artemis, the huntress goddess.

ARCHITECTURAL STYLES
Greek temples were built in two main styles, Doric and Ionic. In Doric temples the columns had tops, called capitals, which were very simple.

The Ionic style columns were more slender and their capitals were decorated with a scroll-like design, called a volute.

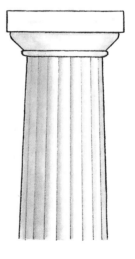

Doric

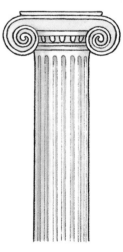

Ionic

The cow is led to the altar for sacrifice, accompanied by young girls holding offering bowls. The herdsman controls the frightened animal.

Another more decorated style was called Corinthian. The capitals were carved in the shape of acanthus leaves. These became very popular in later Roman times.

Corinthian

TEMPLES AND SACRIFICE

Temples were sacred buildings, decorated with carved or moulded sculpture, and regarded as the dwelling places of the gods. People may not have been allowed inside very often.

There was usually a huge statue of the god or goddess to whom the temple was dedicated. In Athens there was a big gold and ivory statue of Athena dressed in armour and looking very awe-inspiring. A special treasury within the temples held precious gifts to the gods.

The altar for sacrificing animals was outside the temple, and it was here in the open air that the citizens gathered on important occasions to make offerings to their patron deity.

DEATH AND BURIAL

Funerals were important events in ancient Greece. The family of the dead person came together to grieve and pray to the gods. The body was prepared for burial with precious sweet smelling oils kept in slender clay oil flasks called *lekythoi*. The *lekythoi* were often decorated with scenes of dead people, especially young soldiers being laid to rest. When the pots were emptied of their oils they were placed on the grave as funeral offerings from the family.

A tall, spindly kind of pot called a *loutrophoros* was used to fill the bath which a young bride took before her wedding. The pots were usually painted with scenes of weddings or funerals. Women who never married had these pots placed as markers over their graves.

MOURNERS

The dead body was laid out on a couch at home and friends and relatives came to pay their respects. A long procession accompanied the dead body to the cemetery which was usually outside the city. A group of women would follow the hearse, weeping and tearing their hair in a ritual act of grief.

Food, drink, pots and jewellery or weapons were often placed in the tomb for the use of the dead person in the next world. Rich people had marble grave slabs, or stone coffins called sarcophagi.

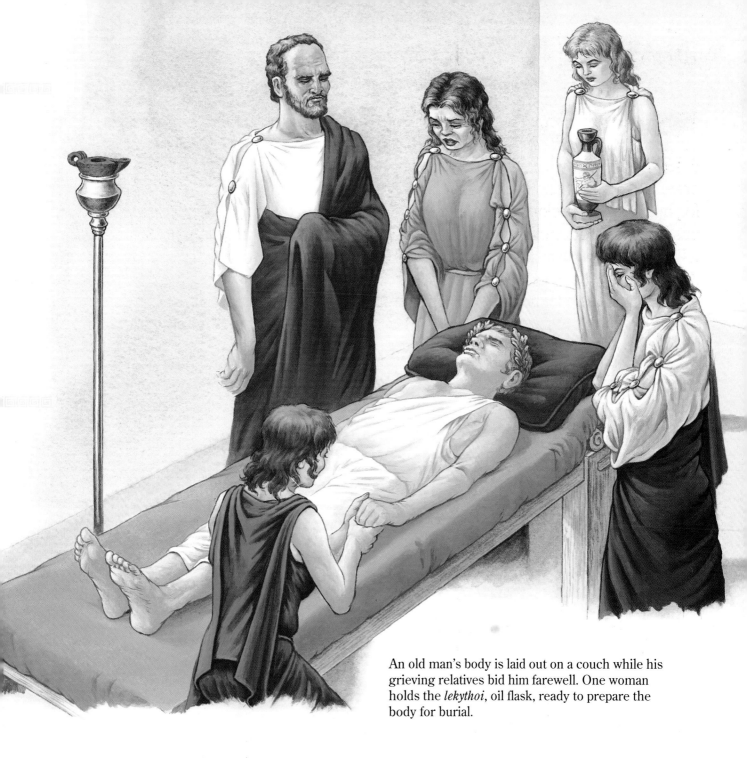

An old man's body is laid out on a couch while his grieving relatives bid him farewell. One woman holds the *lekythoi*, oil flask, ready to prepare the body for burial.

THE AFTERLIFE

The Greeks believed that dead people went to the Underworld, which was ruled by Pluto. They were taken there across the river Styx by a ferryman called Charon. The relatives of the dead person sometimes left a coin on the body as payment to Charon. A wreath was placed on the head of the corpse.

Some Greek gods gave people hope of a life after death. Dionysus, for example, the god of wine, died and was reborn each year. The goddess Persephone came back from the Underworld every year to live with her mother, Demeter, the goddess of the grain harvest, during the spring and summer when the earth flourished.

ANSWERS TO MYSTERY BOXES

Page 14: these clay objects are perfume containers. Whilst these are in the shape of sandalled feet, others have been found in the shape of birds and helmets.

Page 23: it is a strigil or scraper. The sportsmen would rub their bodies with olive oil and then scrape it off, along with any dirt, using these bronze scrapers. This would keep them supple and protect from sunburn.